People Matter Most

The Dirty Little Secrets of Employee Relations & Labor Management

Mason Duchatschek
Jason Greer
Ken Lynch

Table of Contents

People Matter Most

The Dirty Little Secrets of Employee Relations & Labor Management

INTRODUCTION

Managing companies, and in particular managing employees, over the past 20 years has changed dramatically! For starters, think of how the Internet and the use of mobile devices have impacted how employees and potential employees research companies, search for better opportunities, and apply online. And employees and potential employees aren't the only ones using the Internet. Companies are also using the Internet to conduct research on their employees and potential applicants on social media sites – such as LinkedIn, Facebook, My Space, Plaxo, to name a few – in order to find out as much information as they can to ensure they have the "right" hire.

Next, you have the government influencing how companies manage. You have government laws, regulations, rules and policies for everything from starting a company and running the day-to-day operations to recruiting employees and providing adequate pay and benefits for employees to training employees, and even transitioning the employees out of the company (meaning terminating the employee). Everything seems to be regulated these days.

If that isn't enough for company managers to worry about, over the past few years there has been a dramatic increase in union organizing activity throughout the United States. Why the focus on unionization? Unions are a "for profit" organization, and their membership has dramatically decreased over the past 20 years. This means their source of revenue (mainly monthly union dues) has dramatically decreased as well. So in order for the unions to survive, they must raise money every year, just like any business. Simply put, without revenue, they will cease to operate.

Why do unions feel they can be successful and organize YOUR employees? To start, recent federal guidelines on organizing have changed, making it easier for unions to organize. But the biggest reasons why unions feel they can be successful are because they believe employees are dissatisfied at work, their managers are not treating them fairly, their managers won't listen to their concerns, and they aren't being paid enough. What the union is promising is this:

they (the union) will listen to their (the employees') concerns and go to the company, on behalf of the employees, and get them (the employees) better working conditions and more pay.

Please understand, the authors of this book are not anti-union. Quite the contrary. We believe that in some situations, organizations deserve to have a union representing the employees. However, we believe that in most situations, companies are more successful when they have the ability to manage without third-party intervention. And with proper manager training in place, along with a change in how the company treats its employees, there will develop a culture within the organization of trust and mutual respect. And once this culture is identified, it makes it so much easier for the company to hire and retain employees, thus making the company successful, as well as the employees.

Today, companies have many tools available to find the right employees. To get the word out about job openings, companies use Internet posting sites (such as CareerBuilder, Monster and LinkedIn), as well as place the openings on the company's own website; once they are posted, search engines (such as Simply Hired or

Indeed) collect the openings and place them on their own sites. Once applicants are identified, through the use of behavior-based assessments, companies can identify the applicants likely to fit into the organization's culture. And when you hire the right employees, you will likely increase employee satisfaction and engagement, as well as increase retention, decrease turnover and positively impact the bottom-line financials of the organization!

This takes us to the purpose of this book. This book is written for those who handle the day-to-day activities involving the most valuable asset the company has: its employees! You are the company representative who works in the trenches and is involved in dealing with employees, from the application process to hiring to training to disciplining to the day the employee leaves your organization. This book is written with the chief executive, as well as the first-line manager, in mind, providing guidance and direction in managing employees.

This is about unions and the challenges created by bad management. It is also about preventative strategies used by good management teams to solve common business problems before they occur. And you'll also discover how to treat your employees the right way to ensure you have an engaged workforce committed to the success of your organization. In this book, we feel you will find "real world" solutions to "real world" challenges.

You'll find this book written differently than most labor-management books. It was not written like a school textbook or dry management theory book. What we wanted to do was write this book as if we were sitting at a coffee shop, relaxed and informal, discussing labor and management issues and how to be successful in dealing with them. So you'll see much of this book is written in the first person, just as if you were having an informal discussion with one of the authors. Most chapters were written as if you asked one of the authors a question and were there listening to their response. So sit back and get comfortable, grab a cup of coffee, and welcome to our conversation about labor–management relations.

SECTION ONE

"Mason, what are the challenges of management?"

If you own a business or manage employees, you're in a war consisting of multiple battles on several fronts. The stakes are high. There is a battle for the hearts, minds and souls of your employees. There's a battle to gain more customers and to keep the ones you already have, longer. There's a battle to gain and retain the best employees. There's the battle to keep costs down and productivity up. The problem is, these battles are going on simultaneously but you have limited resources to commit to these battles.

Some threats are external. Some are internal. You can see some threats coming, and others are just out of sight. Not all threats are bad. Some are exactly what your company needs right now, more than anything else, to drive the necessary change and help you continue along your path to success.

Chapter 1:
The Easy and Right Approach

More than 20 years ago, when I was a brand-new Second Lieutenant in the Missouri Army National Guard, I had a conversation with Colonel Calvin Broughton that I never forgot. It was about the four ways of getting things accomplished. Colonel Broughton pulled me into his office and grabbed a piece of paper and a pen. He then drew a matrix consisting of two columns and two rows by drawing one big square, with a line going right through the middle from top to bottom and another going through the middle from left to right, to create four smaller squares.

WRONG RIGHT

EASY

HARD

Colonel Broughton told me there was a wrong way to do things and a right way to do things. Then he proceeded to label the first column WRONG and the second column RIGHT.

After that, he told me there were hard ways to do things and easy ways to do things. Then he labeled the top row EASY and the bottom row HARD.

The Colonel pointed out the box where the row he labeled as HARD intersected with the column he labeled as WRONG and told me to avoid spending my time there at all costs, because there is usually tons of work there, and in the end, it is not going to pay off.

He also pointed at the box labeled EASY and WRONG. There is an upside to failing fast, even though it still means failing.

Then he pointed at the box labeled HARD and RIGHT. "That's a tough way to lead because it's resource intensive and it wears out your soldiers, even if you accomplish your mission," he said.

Finally, Col. Broughton pointed to the box where the row he labeled as EASY intersected with the column he labeled RIGHT. I smiled, because I knew that's where the Colonel wanted me to be spending my time. This is where we want to help YOU spend your time, too.

Think about YOUR organization. Do you or your organization struggle with any of the following challenges:

- Possible union organizing activity?

- Employee theft?

- Fraudulent worker's compensation claims?

- Absenteeism?

- Tardiness?

- Overtime costs?

- Substance abuse in your workforce?

- Employee injuries?

- Sales productivity?

- Threats of (or actual) employee lawsuits?

- Employee drama that's killing productivity?

- Unwanted employee turnover?

9

I know, you probably have some good ideas on how to fix at least some of those problems. Given enough time and resources, I'd like to believe that you would accomplish your mission. What we would like for you to do is do it the EASY and RIGHT way.

Want a proactive (EASY) approach to solving (or at least minimizing) the problems listed above?

Address the causes, not the effects, and you can prevent problems before they ever occur.

But remember this: If YOU don't address the causes, if YOU don't address the concerns of your employees, then your employees will look for someone who will. Can you guess who that someone will be? Correct – a union!

Chapter 2:
Unions Want You!

Unions want your employees' trust because they make money collecting billions of dollars each year in dues. They also know that the more members they represent, the more leverage they have and pressure they can apply to companies to get what they want. But it is more than just the money they collect; they also believe passionately in their mission and ability to rescue good people from horrible management.

Employers want their employees' trust because they don't want to lose the autonomy and freedom they have to run their business the way they want, uninterrupted. Many employers also view unions as an unnecessary expense that makes them less competitive, because a union presence doesn't add additional value or cost savings to their bottom line. They complain that union rules and additional bureaucracy protect and overpay lazy employees who barely (and often don't) carry their own weight. Employers want compensation plans that reward productivity as much as, if not more than, seniority. They also want to avoid the risk of negative media attention, lost business revenue and damage to their brand related to future disputes.

Some unions have earned their bad reputations and are even more ruthless than members of the general public and business management teams even realize. Some employers are also more ruthless and heartless than members of the general public (except their own employees) realize.

I am not anti-union, and no one in my family is anti-union. In fact, I had two union jobs myself, during high school and college. While I was in high school, I worked as a union employee stocking shelves, running a cash register and bagging groceries for a supermarket chain. I think I made $4.50 per hour when the minimum wage was $3.35. Then, during the summer between my freshman and sophomore years in college, I had a summer job at a union bottling plant and made $9.35 per hour when the minimum wage was still $3.35.

When I was a little boy, during the summer months my parents made the 500-mile drive from their home in St. Louis to Oshkosh, Wisconsin, so my brother and I could spend a week visiting our grandparents. My grandfather, Leo Duchatschek, had an eighth grade education and worked in a Rockwell factory for over 40 years. It was a union job. It paid well and provided my grandfather with benefits, allowing him to raise five children and live comfortably until his passing at the age of 95. I can still remember getting up early so I could ride with my grandmother as she drove Grandpa to the factory for work. I remember sitting in the station wagon with the windows down, parked across the street from the factory in the late afternoon summer heat, waiting for Grandpa to get off work.

Ironically, only a few years ago, I was invited by the University of Wisconsin in Oshkosh to speak to a group of their local business leaders. As I was preparing to leave the parking lot after that speaking engagement, something seemed eerily familiar. It was then I realized I was standing just down the street from the factory where my grandfather had worked for over 40 years. It is ironic how things happen. Here I was, the first Duchatschek to graduate from college, speaking at the college next to where my grandfather worked for so many years.

In a perfect world, we don't think unions would be necessary. In a perfect world, employees and employers could work together happily. Both groups would feel they were being treated fairly by the other. There would be mutual respect for each other.

Unfortunately, we don't live in a perfect world. But there is good news! There are ways to improve the environment within your organization. It is our hope that the ideas, strategies and tools we discuss in this book will help you and your organization move closer to that ideal relationship. Think about some of these issues that impact the environment within your organization:

1. What is the key to avoiding a union organizing threat? Take good care of the people who take care of your business. Treat them fairly. Reward them and express appreciation for their contributions. Give them a voice and listen to what they have to say. Keep them safe. Communicate kindly and compassionately. Treat them with respect.

2. Want to reduce employee theft and fraudulent worker's compensation? Hire (and retain) honest people who won't steal or lie about being hurt to get paid without having to work. (Hint: You can measure the presence or absence of integrity before you hire them.)

3. Want to reduce overtime costs related to absenteeism and/or tardiness? Hire (and retain) people who are reliable. (Hint: You can measure reliability before you hire them.)

4. Want to reduce substance abuse in your workforce and injuries related to it? Hire (and retain) people who don't use drugs. (Hint: Physical drug testing isn't always enough, but there are other ways to screen for drug-free attitudes.)

5. Want to increase sales? Hire (and retain) people who can sell.

   Are you starting to see a pattern here?

6. Want to minimize risks associated with lawsuits, productivity-killing employee conflict and drama, employee turnover and more? Hire (and retain) people who match

the demands of the job, and make sure they work well with the manager/supervisor who leads them. (Hint: We will talk in detail about how to do this later, so hang in there.)

SECTION TWO

"Jason, can you tell us more about labor relations and unions?"

Employees aren't likely to seek a third party to represent them if they feel that their needs and interests are currently being represented within the organization. As a former board agent for the National Labor Relations Board, and as a consultant hired by management, whenever I reflect on all of the union organizing drives I've been a part of, the core issue nine out of ten times is people being treated poorly by management. If management doesn't improve, a union will be back, making it that much harder to beat them the next time.

Some questions you may want to ask are: "What happens if your organization isn't anywhere close to the ideal employee–management relationship?" "What if your organization was there at one time but is now moving in the wrong direction?" "What if things are going great and you want to keep it that way?"

Maybe your workforce is already unionized. Maybe it isn't, but you are paving the way for your existing labor force to make that move. And if it isn't, maybe you want to make sure it stays that way.

You will have important choices to make. There will be rewards or consequences tied to each of them. But be aware: while the rewards may be large, the consequences may be just as significant.

Chapter 3:
Labor Relations – Seizing Opportunities or Facing the Consequences

I don't believe employees should be "denied" their right to union representation. I don't believe employers should be denied their right to make the case against unionization to their employees.

There is an old labor relations maxim that says, "People don't vote for a union, they vote against bad management." That may be true, but I happen to exist in a world that believes all problems can be fixed. It's important to remind employers and employees that they need each other.

Sure, people will work for money, but they will die for respect and recognition. Without respect, there is no loyalty. And that is a two-way street.

Since the advent of the National Labor Relations Act, new laws and regulations have come and gone. Corporations have traditionally been given more power during Republican administrations and have seen their powers reduced when Democrats occupied the Oval Office.

The kind of change I would like to see in labor relations has nothing to do with revamping laws or critiquing things such as how unions go about reporting their earnings to the Department of Labor. In fact, I could care less.

What I do care about are employees. I care about that single mother who is working two jobs just to be able to purchase groceries for her children. I care about that hardworking day laborer who scratches and claws just to break even in a world that tells him that his skills are becoming a thing of the past. I care about the managers and leaders responsible for achieving a healthy bottom line and profit so the company providing all the jobs to ALL the people, BOTH management and labor, continues to exist.

Chapter 4:
Unions – What You're Up Against

Historically speaking, if not for labor unions we would not have many of the things that we actually take for granted today. It is unlikely a workweek would be defined as 40 hours. Many workers would not have had the quality benefit packages they've enjoyed in the past. Equal pay requirements most likely wouldn't have been put into place when they were. And rights for ethnic minorities, as well as women, would not be where they are today if it weren't for the contributions of unions.

This is the 21st century. Businesses and employees want to know, "What have you done for me lately?" Other questions being asked now are questions like this: "Are labor unions affecting our business in a positive way? If so, how? If not, why not?" When you think about it, if labor unions did a better job making a business case for their existence, companies would be lining up at their doors saying, "Help us help our employees." *from ~1 stewards?*

The labor relations field literally went into existence the moment the National Labor Relations Act was created in 1935. As labor unions emerged and grew, "labor relations consultants" emerged to counter union activities on behalf of business management teams.

The role of the labor relations consultant in the 1930s was – and still is to this very day – to educate employees so that they will not join a union. There are many techniques that quality consultants will use to drive their point home, but their #1 responsibility is ensuring that the majority of employees vote "No" when it comes time to decide on becoming part of a unionized workforce.

Labor relations is the field of study that looks at the relationship between employees and employers and whether a union currently represents those employees or not. The National Labor Relations Act governs the field of labor relations and establishes and manages the rules by which unions and employers present their case to employees who are considering unionization.

The National Labor Relations Board (NLRB) governs the National Labor Relations Act. Simply put, the National Labor Relations Act says employees have the right to organize collectively as a group and negotiate the terms and conditions of employment with the employer.

The sole focus of the National Labor Relations Board is to make sure that the National Labor Relations Act is properly applied. The National Labor Relations Board serves two primary functions. One is to prevent and remedy unfair labor practices. The second is to establish, usually through a secret ballot election, whether or not employees want to be part of a union.

Generally speaking, when a union is looking at organizing within a company, they will go to the National Labor Relations Board and file a certification petition. It lets the employer know the union wishes to represent their employees.

What most businesses don't know, and find out the hard way, is that when they've been hit by a petition, the union has been working on their people anywhere from a year to a year and a half. It was taking place right under their noses.

Additionally, the union has done their homework. Union leaders have uncovered what they need to know about all of your employees. They know which managers are popular and which ones aren't. They understand the flow of your business and what it takes to operate it.

Unfortunately, union leaders often understand employee wants and needs BETTER than the managers supposedly leading the employees each day. How? It's because the employees are reaching outside of their organization and talking to a third party (the union) about their issues instead of their managers.

Chapter 5:
How Unions Make Money

Since unions do not supply tangible goods, where do they make their money? They make their money from convincing employees to join the labor union and pay dues. The dues are fees that employees pay to have the union represent them when negotiating with their employer. Union leaders negotiate the terms and conditions of employment contracts between a unionized group of employees and the employer. Most union contracts are binding for a period of three to five years (while some can be eight to ten years in duration) and pertain to wages; terms of employment and working conditions are clearly defined in the contract. Unions continue to receive dues for the entire duration of the contract they negotiate with an employer. Because each employee represents a dollar sign, that's why unions push so hard to represent them.

Unions are constantly doing online searches for companies that have:

1. Gone through acquisitions

2. Had a series of layoffs

3. Recorded positive profits

4. Been struggling

Throughout the country, unions are targeting companies every day. They are targeting specific industries. They are looking for a vulnerable moment. If you're making "too much money," they will attempt to convince your employees they aren't getting their "fair share" and deserve more. If you've been struggling, stressed-out managers with limited resources might increase demands on workers, upping the stress level that goes with it. Unions will be ready to step in and make the case that they can improve working conditions and teach management a lesson. If employees don't believe in you, they'll be much more receptive to the next person (usually a union rep) telling them what they want to hear.

Chapter 6:
Stages of Unionization

There are three stages of unionization. The first stage is the organization stage. The second stage is the negotiation stage. The third stage is the contract settlement/dispute stage.

Organization

In the organization stage, the focus of the union is directed toward getting your employees to sign what they call union authorization cards. When the union gets at least 30% of your employees to sign these union authorization cards or to sign some type of petition, that's when they have the right to go to the National Labor Relations Board (NLRB) and file a petition. Once the petition has been filed, your company is under an active union organizing threat.

In the past, the time between when the union filed a petition with the NLRB and the actual secret ballot election to accept or reject unionization by the employees was about 42 days. The NLRB has the power and authority to extend this period of time or REDUCE it dramatically.

Because unions typically begin "working" an employee base 12–18 months before a petition is filed with the NLRB, it is difficult for an employer to convince employees to vote against a union in only 42 days. Can you imagine how much harder it would be for an employer to make their case in a FRACTION of that time? The less time an employer has, the harder it is to make their case and try to refute whatever lies and false promises the union has ingrained in the minds of employees during the last year or year and a half.

Negotiation

If the union wins the vote in the secret ballot election, then we proceed to the second stage. It's known as negotiation. It is also referred to by some as the collective bargaining process. During this time, representatives from the company and the union attempt to "negotiate in good faith" on issues such as who can work and who can't work for the company, wages, working conditions, the discipline process, grievance procedures, health and welfare and pension premiums and the duties of the shop steward in handling employee issues, just to name a few.

Contract Settlement/Dispute

The third stage is either a contract settlement or a dispute. Settlement means the employer and the union have agreed to the terms and conditions of a labor contract, the collective bargaining agreement (CBA). If there's a dispute, it simply means that the union and the company haven't been able to come to an agreement yet and the union has either decided to take the employees out on strike or the company has decided to lock out their employees.

IS this an option in an already-existing unionized workplace trying to negotiate future contracts?

Chapter 7:
The Cast of Characters

There are many individuals involved in the organization attempt within a company: the union organizer, the internal organizer, "salts," outside consultants and the company's own management defense team. All the individuals involved have an interest in the outcome of the union vote; thus, all will work very hard and do whatever it takes to reach the outcome they want.

The Union Organizer

I think it is fair to say that unions are motivated to collect dues from their members. After all, unions take in billions of dollars a year from dues, fees, appropriations, etc. They know it's easy money, too, since management often fails to properly handle and care for the needs of line-level employees. It's also fair to say that they believe in their mission as well.

Union organizers, both at the local and international level, range in shape and size. Some have formal educations. Others are street-smart and have lots of relevant and valuable experience.

Regardless of their responsibilities or backgrounds, organizers believe all employees desire to be treated with respect and dignity and that THEY, not the company's management team, best know how to care for and work with employees. Organizers also believe the CBA is the best way to help oppressed employees everywhere, and many of them feel like it is their job to save the world.

Passion and commitment to their cause are what give them the audacity to stand outside of your building with their picket signs and leaflets, dig through your trash looking for intel, hire moles/secret agents, also known as "salts," to infiltrate your company and gather the inside information they need to turn the will of your people against you and more. They don't believe your management team deserves to interact with your employees without a union representative being present. They want to change the world, business-by-business, employee-by-employee. Management, in their eyes, is nothing more than the sacrificial lamb on the altar of equality and justice.

It is way too easy to cast a unionizer using thuggish stereotypes. It's true that some of them have mastered the art of intimidation and aren't afraid to demonstrate that particular skill set, especially with management consultants. (I've experienced death threats, slashed tires, ransacked hotel rooms and more.) However, it is also important to realize that you are selling them short if you write them off as mere bullies or thugs. It has been my experience that the best union organizers are very intelligent and empathetic people. They also have been taught how to understand the hearts, minds and souls of the employees they're trying to organize.

The union organizers know that RESPECT is what employees want most often, even more than extra money. Experienced organizers know that they are competing with an employer to show respect because that is the linchpin in almost every campaign.

The knee-jerk reaction for some employers is to tell their employees things like, "Don't join the union. Unions are bad. The union's just here to steal your money." They don't realize how committed union organizers are to offering employees "a voice" and a "seat at the table" with management.

The Internal Organizer

Unions are always looking for what they call an internal organizer. The internal organizer is a hard-line, pro-union employee who is passionate about the union cause. This is a person who is willing to supply the union with as much information as they possibly can about the company and the people who manage it.

Why would an employee want to become an internal organizer for the union? Some are passionate about the cause. Others are angry at management.

Unions know the only way they win is if a majority of the people who voted during the secret ballot election choose to unionize. It is a numbers game to the union organizer. When the union has an effective internal organizer working for them, the company will have a much more difficult time defeating the union.

The "Salts"

What is a "salt"? "Salting" is the process by which a union will train an individual to appear as an ideal job candidate, but they are really more like a mole or double agent once they make it through the typical 30-, 60- or 90-day probationary period. Their only goal is to get a job at your company and help the union organize your workers.

The Consultants/Management's Defense Team

Although the means of educating employees has changed (videos and PowerPoint presentations are the new norm), the qualifications of the consultants representing management have not changed much over the years. The majority of consultants are (a) ex-union members, (b) former NLRB agents, (c) human resource professionals, (d) attorneys and (e) anyone who offers some type of needed attribute to the management campaign, such as being able to speak a foreign language or having previously worked within the industry that is being organized by a union.

The field of consultants representing management is full of intelligent men and women. Like their union counterparts, the field of labor relations consultants also has its share of bullies. Many consultants feel that their mission in life is to expose hypocrisy and lies in the union movement and don't mind being paid handsomely for doing it.

Former union members who leave union employment to become consultants are often hell-bent on fighting against their former unions, and they know firsthand that the unions they are competing with will do "whatever it takes" to win. Unfortunately, because that was how they were taught, they simply bring their "whatever it takes" attitudes to the other side and support management. It's a double-edged sword.

Yes, they help win elections against unions, and that sounds good to business management teams in the short term. However, in the long run, it has been my experience that too many of the former union members advising management teams lack training on what to do after the election. They often ended up leaving the company they represented in disarray, and the problems the union promised to help fix didn't go away. The needs of the employees were still being ignored, and management went right back to doing the same things that opened the door to the unions in the first place.

The main objective for the consultants who represent management is to defeat the union by getting the majority of employees to vote against joining a union when it comes time to vote. The good consultants are equally concerned with helping management learn from their mistakes and make the necessary changes and improvements in the way they operate. Once management makes the necessary changes, happy employees won't be as receptive when a union tries to convince them to try organizing a second or even a third time.

Chapter 8:
Common Organizing Strategies and Tactics

In union organizing campaigns, I have seen some despicable behavior. Members of business management teams have made poor behavioral choices, just as some people representing the unions have.

There are some fundamental union organizing strategies and tactics that are very common, and every management team needs to be aware of them. Why? Because business management teams are usually the ones under attack.

You are naive to believe that union reps are simply standing outside your door telling employees that management stinks, doesn't care and underpays. It goes much deeper. They know how to make things personal.

Making Things Personal

If the average union spends 12 to 18 months "working" your employees before a petition gets filed, you must know that they are studying more than your employee base. Rest assured they have invested that time studying management as well. They know which managers are popular and which ones aren't. Having that knowledge gives the union the ability to push an employee's hot buttons, incite emotional reactions and manipulate pro-union sentiment much more easily and effectively.

For example, consider the real-life case of a successful electronics company. The owner of the company lived a real-life rags-to-riches story. He only had about an eighth grade education. However, through hard work and perseverance, he built up what became a $50 million dollar operation from scratch.

Many of the people in his warehouse were people who had been with him from day one. They saw the transformation before their eyes. The same man whom they remember sleeping in the back of his truck was now being chauffeured to work every day in his beautiful Bentley. The workers felt the owner had lost touch with them and had begun seeing them less as friends and "brothers in the struggle" and more as disposable units of labor.

You know how Linus from the Charlie Brown cartoons always used to carry his blanket? Well, this guy used to carry a Louisville Slugger baseball bat. He carried it everywhere, including the warehouse. He walked up and down the warehouse aisles every day. He usually didn't say much, just stared and kept moving.

If he noticed something he didn't like or felt an employee was slacking off, he'd stop and tap the bat on the employee's right shoulder. He didn't tap anyone hard enough to cause pain, but he did tap hard enough to get an employee's undivided attention. In his mind, his actions were showing employees he cared, was paying attention and appreciated it when things were done correctly.

As you can imagine, his employees didn't take it that way. They felt they were being diminished and threatened. It scared them. Even the employees who had been with him since day one felt like he had lost touch. Newer employees were just afraid of the guy with the bat and of losing their jobs.

It didn't take long for the employees to reach out to a labor union. The labor union was glad to get involved and began gathering the information they thought they needed to wage a successful campaign against the company.

Union representatives stood outside the owner's facility every day passing out brochures, also known as handbills. The first handbill happened to show a picture of the owner of the company, holding his bat, with a tagline that said, "How long is it going to take before he starts to beat you like a wounded dog?"

This angered the owner. However, he didn't do anything about it.

The second day, the union reps passed out different handbills featuring pictures of his beautiful, luxurious mansion and his chauffeured Bentley. It angered him more, but he still didn't do anything.

The third day, the handbills featured pictures of his beautiful wife. More specifically, the pictures were particularly complimentary of her cosmetic breast-enhancement surgery. Under the photographs featuring her breasts, the union reps wrote, "Look at what your hard work bought the owner's wife."

This is what I mean about a union's ability and desire to target management teams and individuals at a personal level. Nothing is sacred or off-limits.

At that point, the owner had had enough. He passionately grabbed his bat and was on his way to "have some words" with the union reps he felt were antagonizing, harassing and embarrassing him.

Unknown to him was the fact that he was being set up the whole time. The union reps were waiting for this and had hidden cameras set up to catch the craziness they knew would unfold on video. Needless to say, the union reps just laughed at him while he ran after them with his bat. It only made him madder and more animated on video.

Warehouse employees started sharing the video with their friends and family members. The union sent it to the owner's customers, community leaders and local media outlets. The headlines were about a local business owner who had gone crazy.

Again, nothing is sacred or off-limits when it comes to union strategies and tactics. The union knew exactly what they had to do to provoke him on a personal level, and they did a heck of a job at it.

Lying by Omission and Truth Manipulation

Unions are known to lie by omission and manipulate the truth. Allow me to give you an example.

Over the past few years, unions have done their part to perpetuate and amplify perceived differences between the "haves" and have-nots in our society. They know that perception equals reality, and they are very skilled at creating and orchestrating perceptions of their own creation.

They will attempt to empathize with your employees. They will ask your employees if it's fair that management can easily provide a nice life for their families and send their kids to college while the employees are working long hours just to keep their mortgage and utility bills paid and food on the table. Unions will also suggest that the shareholders are making more money, literally taking money out of the employees' pockets, and then ask employees how long they plan to take the scraps left over from the managers' tables.

Unions know when line employees lack business knowledge. As part of their research, they identify employees who know their jobs and work hard but lack a basic understanding of fundamental business and economic principles. They prey upon these people and exploit them.

For example, if your company generated 15 million dollars in REVENUE last quarter, a union rep might go to employees who they know won't know any better and say things like, "If the company made 15 million dollars last quarter, why can't you get a raise?" They mislead employees to mistakenly think you actually made 15 million dollars in PROFIT. They don't bother to explain how expenses like taxes, depreciation, equipment maintenance, salaries and benefits all have to be taken out. It makes you, as an employer, sound much greedier and unfair when unions tell your employees that you made 15 million and won't give them a raise, rather than actually telling the whole truth and explaining that your company barely broke even last quarter.

Pre-Election Promises

Unions make pre-election promises. It's not like the employees can change their votes after the union has been put in place.

An online grocery distributor with about 900 employees had an interesting situation: two different unions were competing against each other to represent their employees. Because the client was in the food/grocery industry, the United Food and Commercial Workers (UFCW) sought to represent these employees. Because so many employees worked in warehouse operations, the International Brotherhood of Teamsters sought to represent them as warehouse employees. To settle the conflict, the National Labor Relations Board (NLRB) just went ahead and ruled that the employees were going to have an opportunity to vote as to whether they wanted to be part of the UFCW, the Teamsters or neither.

Because the company ran three different shifts as a 24-hour operation, the UFCW and the Teamsters had representatives there around the clock. Whatever the employees said they wanted, the union would "guarantee" that's what they were going to get. They would say things like, "If you want $5 more an hour, come vote for the UFCW." When the Teamsters heard that, the Teamsters would counter with, "But if you want $7 an hour, come vote for us."

It got to the point where reps from both unions were making any and every promise they possibly could in order to entice employees to vote for their particular union. In that campaign, the employees knew they were being lied to, scammed and manipulated, so they rejected both unions.

Regrettably, it doesn't always work that way, and far too many groups of employees DO put their faith in false promises. The groups of employees who learn this lesson the hard way don't realize until after it's too late that they can't take their votes back once the union, who lied to them, is in place.

Physical Presence

One of the most obvious tactics unions use is standing outside your facility so they can talk to workers and pass out fliers and other propaganda. But remember, they aren't just standing there. They are also watching *everything* that is going on.

One tactic that unions often employ that businesses don't anticipate or prepare for, even though they should, is dumpster diving. Yes, union reps will dig through your trash. They are looking for ANYTHING they can use against your company. They will grab and analyze reams of paper. (Note : Unless you want to make their job easier, you should shred all your paperwork before you throw it away. Some union reps will even invest time in trying to put the shredded paper back together!)

It is also important to protect your electronic data and information. Union reps have proven themselves incredibly adept and capable of launching "cyber attacks" and other means of gathering company files. Once they have those files, they will be analyzing everything they can about your employees, your management team or any company-related financials.

Home Visits

Another tactic used by unions is the home visit. This is most popular during the organizing stage.

This is not usually "in your face" effort to sell the benefits of unionization. In fact, it's almost the opposite. Union reps are courting "friendship" and attempting to build relationships and trust with your employees. Union reps will do whatever they can to ingratiate themselves with your employees. They will connect via social media accounts, carry on text message conversations and visit via cell phone, too, just like real friends do.

I recall hearing that during an in-home visit, one employee was confiding in his new "friend" (the union rep) that he and his wife hadn't gone out on a date in so long that his wife was complaining. The union rep gave him some cash, told the employee to take her somewhere nice and volunteered to babysit.

How do you think the employee felt? Not only did his new "friend" babysit his kids, but he also gave him money to take his wife out on a date! WOW! His new "friend" obviously cared more about him than the employer, right? Why wouldn't the employee want to give his new "friend" the opportunity to represent him as an employee?

Community Events

Consider the case of a parking facility in a major metropolitan market. The majority of the employees of the facility were Ethiopian.

The union targeting this company looked around the country until they found the only Ethiopian union organizer they could find. Once they found him, they shipped him into town, and for the better part of a year he hung out within the Ethiopian community. He knew where the employees went to church. He invited them out to community events. He would meet them at Starbucks or wherever else they were hanging out.

It got to the point where this guy stopped being perceived as a union organizer and everyone thought of him as a "friend." This made it possible for him to present himself as a true ally to the employees. He wanted them to feel like they were joining a greater cause, rather than a union.

He put in the time necessary, and the parking company had no idea what they were really up against.

Churching

Consider the case of a steel company I helped in a small town. I noticed during the first week of the campaign that the majority of employees seemed to be anti-union. Initially, they wanted nothing to do with paying dues.

As the days went by, employees' attitudes toward me and toward the other consultants started to change. They started saying things I'd never heard before like, "I think Jesus wants us to join the union." I had no idea how to argue with people who believed that Jesus now wanted them to join the union.

A few days later, a very kind older gentleman invited me to church. It felt awkward, so I tried to tactfully decline. He persisted and insisted that there were things happening "right now that I needed to be aware of."

Sunday came and I met him at church. The congregation, just like the majority of the labor force at the steel company, was African-American. Let's just say that the church service wasn't the meditative or reflective type. People were clapping, singing and dancing in the pews as they experienced the Holy Spirit. The pastor had a fiery style and emotional way of delivering his message that held the people in the congregation totally captivated.

Now, while this spirited and highly energetic service was going on, I also noticed four white males sitting in the back corner of the sanctuary wearing jackets that read "U.S. Steel Workers." Needless to say, you couldn't miss seeing them.

As the pastor began to conclude his sermon, he looked around and said, "I know that there are many of you in this congregation today who are struggling with the decision about whether or not to join the union at the local steel factory. I just want you to know that God will be with you in your decision. I'd also like to take the time to say 'thank you' to the four gentlemen in the back and extend a special thanks to their union for donating $30,000 to our missions. Because of their support, we are now able to send three of our missionaries overseas. I also want to thank them for the additional $10,000 contribution they made so we can build a new playground for the church."

This is what the kind older gentleman wanted me to see for myself. The potential voters for the union, through the words of their own pastor, thought Jesus wanted them to join the union.

Salting/The Use of Salts

What is "salting"? Most businesses have no idea what a "salt" is. When they find out, it's usually too late to do anything about it. When a salt succeeds, employers become unionized.

The salt is instructed to perform as a "good, not great" employee. The union wants their salt (mole/secret agent) to make it through probation and get hired full-time without drawing too much attention to themselves or standing out too much.

The salt is there for one reason and one reason only. They are there to organize your facility for the union. On the surface, they appear to do a good job, and managers like them because they accomplish assigned tasks.

Behind the scenes and outside of the watchful eyes of management, they are collecting information on your employees. They are collecting information on your management team members. They are collecting information on your organization. And they are supplying all that information to the union.

Salting is real. Salting is powerful. Salting is real powerful.

Here's an example: I was consulting for a company that had just opened up a brand-new facility. They were in a rush to hire as many employees as they possibly could. To their credit, they did decent background checks. However, in their rush to get people hired, they weren't as thorough as they perhaps should have been. They unknowingly hired a salt.

The local union sent in numerous salts to apply, until one of those salts was actually hired. The salt got a job as a truck driver, got through probation and became a full-time employee.

According to the employees, the salt spent a lot of time asking them questions about their personal lives and how they felt about management. They didn't know it until later, but he also spent a lot of time listening and documenting as well.

After five months on the job, the salt was involved in an accident. He turned over a company truck and did over $125,000 in damage. Because he was a "good employee," the company didn't terminate him. Instead, they put him in the office and made him an assistant to his manager.

The salt had open access to everything including employee records, company financial information and more. He gathered as much relevant information as he could possibly gather and turned it all over to the union. The salt's main purpose was to turn the facility on its head, and he succeeded.

A few months later the company got hit with the bad news. A petition had been filed, and the union was going to have the opportunity to organize their employees.

The bad news got worse. Why? The company had no idea how much damage had already been done to their employee relations. They didn't have time to undo the damage and refute propaganda.

The union had that campaign won before the petition was ever filed. It wasn't because the company did anything that horribly wrong. The bottom line was that the union had so much knowledge about everything that mattered that they had only to push the right buttons at the right times, and they did exactly that.

SECTION THREE

"Mason, what can a company do to stay union-free?"

The easiest way to stay union free is to treat your employees with dignity and respect. I know it sounds so simple, but when employees do not feel respected, they will look for someone WHO WILL treat them with respect. Do you remember the Golden Rule, to treat others as you would like to be treated? Think about it. How would YOU like to be treated?

Chapter 9:
Great Management Makes Unions Unnecessary

Unions feed on friction, bad management and chaos. If you eliminate friction and bad management and are able to keep things running smoothly and quietly, then it is going to be difficult for unions to sink their teeth into your organization.

Yes, unions typically "work" employees for 12 to 18 months before they are able to get a petition filed with the NLRB. However, good employees who like, value and appreciate good leadership and management teams have the opportunity to see how good they have things every day, every week and every year. As long as things are "going great," it's likely they will be reluctant to risk "messing things up" by bringing in a third party.

Reducing Friction – Employee Turnover

Sure, hiring mistakes are expensive. It takes time to advertise a job opening, screen resumes, pay recruiters, interview, onboard and train new employees. As a rule of thumb, you should estimate that your cost of turnover is about 30% of the annual salary of every employee you replace. And for some positions, the turnover costs could reach as high as 200%!

How many W-2s did you put out last year? How many employees do you have currently? Multiply the difference by 30% of your average salary, and you have an estimate of your cost of turnover.

In fact, we challenge you to find out how big of a problem it really is. Do the math. Find out for yourself. Is it a $10,000 problem each year? Is it a $100,000 problem? Is it a million-dollar problem or worse?

Regardless of the result, what if someone was embezzling that amount from your company or department each year? Would you continue ignoring the problem? If so, for how long? Of course you wouldn't ignore the problem. You would take immediate action to stop the losses.

Truth be told, I'm not convinced that your biggest expense comes from employees who leave and have to be replaced. Consider those who are allowed to STAY because they know how to do enough to avoid getting fired – barely. When a slacker remains on a team, a precedent is set, and other employees notice how little effort from a worker management will accept in exchange for a paycheck. Other employees also notice how much "productivity-killing drama" employers will put up with.

When this happens in your company, you forfeit the opportunity cost of replacing one barely productive employee clogging a roster spot with a superstar. Additionally, you also forfeit the opportunity cost of all the other capable employees who dial back their discretionary effort because they know they can.

One of my favorite business books of all time is *Good to Great* by Jim Collins. I wasn't the only one who liked it. In fact, there were so many other people who liked it that it became a best seller and is still read widely around the world.

Collins made the case – successfully, I might add – that the most important thing managers can do is get the right people onto the right seats on their bus (the bus being their company) and get the wrong people off their bus. He argued that it was even more important than having the right business strategy. Why? According to Collins, if you have the right people and they're in the right seats, they'll figure out the best strategy.

Even though that book was written years ago, it's not hard to find managers and executives who still invest time in talking about the key concepts even today. Why? Because they know related mistakes can cost their companies money, ruin their careers and cause loads of personal embarrassment. And as good as Collins's book is, it fails to deliver the answers to some very important questions, such as, how do you get the right people on the bus, and how do you know what the right seats are for each of them?

Other questions that come to mind include: What type of line employees have you brought into your organization? What type of managers have you brought into your organization? Are the needs and the skills of the employees an exact match with the competences and personalities of the management team you put in place? If not, you will have friction. Given enough friction and enough time, employees will actively look outside your organization for help.

We will do our best to answer those questions, introduce you to some of the proven strategies, tactics and tools you might need to pull it all off and show you how to minimize friction.

What separates those who succeed in a job from those who struggle? As mentioned earlier, it's two things. It is the match between a person and the requirements of a job, and the quality of the relationship between an employee and their leader.

Let's talk about the fit between a person and their job first. We can discuss the relationship between an individual and their leader later on.

Chapter 10:
What Separates High-Risk and High-Reward Employees?

Early in my career, and before his passing, I had a conversation with the great Bill Brooks, a well-respected sales trainer and author from North Carolina. In a general sense, he observed over the course of his career that the differences between those who matched their jobs and those who did not fell into three categories.

The first category is SKILL. In other words, you want to know if an individual CAN perform the duties of the job. Does a computer programmer know how to write computer code? Does a lifeguard know how to swim? Does a salesperson know how to present, solve problems and answer objections? Do people interacting with customers have an adequate vocabulary, do they know how to spell and do they possess the basic math skills necessary to make change at a cash register?

Just because an individual has a high school diploma, it does not mean they have an education. Why? It's because there are plenty of schools across the country that aren't accredited. And when you hire an individual who lacks the basic skills, your customers aren't as likely to ask what's wrong with that individual as they are to ask what's wrong with YOUR company. Why? Because to them, that individual IS your company.

The second category is ATTITUDE and VALUES. In other words, you want to know if a person WILL perform their duties and WHY. Do they have integrity, a solid work ethic and reliability? And does their job give them what they value and want most out of a job?

An individual can have all the ability and skill to do a job, but if they don't show up, or show up on time, or put forth the effort to apply their skill, what good is it? If the job doesn't give an individual what they want and value most, beyond the paycheck, then how likely are they to stay or give the maximum of their discretionary effort?

The third category is BEHAVIOR. In other words, you want to know HOW a person performs their duties. An individual can have all the skill and motivation to do a job, but if the job requires them to behave in ways that aren't normal for them, then you can't assume they will actually DO what they know they should be doing, even if they want to.

Does an individual have a strong social need (extroverted), or would they prefer to be left alone (introverted)? Are they rigid or flexible? Are they assertive or passive? Are they calm or hyper? Are they overly trusting or cynical? Are they sensitive or insensitive?

You need to know the answers to these questions BEFORE you hire an external candidate or promote an internal candidate. For example, let's pretend that you have a top-performing line employee and their latest performance appraisal is a glowing report. It says they know their job inside and out. (They have the SKILLS.) They are never late, work hard and have been with the company a long time. (They have the right ATTITUDE and VALUES.) And when it comes to BEHAVIOR, they do what they are told (passive) to do, don't question authority (overly trusting) and work hard to get along with everybody (high social need). They might even be viewed as a team player (overly sensitive) because they are so willing to take into account everyone else's feelings. In this example of a line employee, their behavioral traits are an excellent match to their job.

Think about how many times you have heard managers try to make the case that a person like that should be promoted to supervisor or manager. After all, as the argument is made, they are an ideal employee, and hopefully they will be able to teach everyone else to become the kind of outstanding line employee they are.

Unfortunately, there's a problem. The exact same behavioral traits that contribute to the individual's glowing performance appraisal as a line employee would be the EXACT SAME behavioral traits that would be likely to DOOM him or her as a supervisor. Skill, attitude and values are great, but behaviorally speaking, the supervisory role would require this individual to come to work every day and behave in a way that's not normal or natural for them. It doesn't allow them to be themselves.

In this example, if this individual was promoted into management, how easy would it be for them to take charge (when they are passive)? How would they feel about stepping up to discipline "friends," who used to be coworkers, when they really just want everyone to like them (high social need)? Would they hesitate to offer needed criticism even if it meant hurting someone's feelings (in spite of their own sensitive tendencies)? Would former peers take advantage of their overly trusting nature to get away with things they shouldn't?

You see, it's not enough for an individual to know what to do if their job requires them to consistently behave in ways that don't reflect their own natural behavioral style. Of course, many people do this every day and have for a long time. Unfortunately, they end up hating their jobs and experience an abundance of stress.

This behavioral mismatch causes friction. Friction causes job dissatisfaction. Job dissatisfaction leads to employee turnover, continued poor individual performance, ineffective leadership and, sometimes, successful union organizing campaigns.

When people are matched to jobs that fit their skills, give them what they want most and allow them to be themselves, they're happier. Happy employees are MUCH less likely to leave jobs they love (unless there is friction with their leader, which we will discuss later). They are much less likely to sue when they're happy. And the seeds of discontent that union organizers attempt to spread have a MUCH harder time taking root when people aren't dissatisfied in their roles.

Chapter 11:
Matching a Person to the Job

So, what is the age-old recruiting question? It is this: "How do you match a person with the demands of the job?" I acknowledge that hiring the right person the first time around is easier said than done. If it wasn't, I suspect Jim Collins would have addressed it in his best-selling book *Good to Great* when he decided to write it.

I once had a client who was expressing frustration because he realized that using his traditional employee selection processes, he made good hiring decisions as well as bad ones. Because of his mixed results, the only thing he knew for sure was that his current methods couldn't help him predict, with any reasonable degree of certainty, the likelihood of success.

When it comes to hiring, your decisions are only as sound as the information on which they are based. Failure to utilize every opportunity that is legally available to you to gather relevant, job-related information about your applicants is like agreeing to play Russian roulette without checking all the chambers in the weapon first.

My friend Syd Robinson used to joke that resumes belonged in the library, listed under fiction, mainly because they were nothing more than balance sheets with no liabilities. Experts usually agree that about one-third of resumes are embellished. I have also heard others claim that as many as 70% of employment applications contain lies, distortions or half-truths. Between the lies people tell on their applications and exaggerations on their resumes, only a fraction of the information managers have is reliable.

For the sake of discussion, let's say it's half. The problem is knowing which half. No wonder interviewing is a crapshoot and unprepared interviewers end up making offers to people they like only to find out later their "gut feeling" was wrong.

Background Checks

Performing background checks on applicants can identify people with criminal records and minimize your risk of negligent hiring lawsuits. What are negligent hiring lawsuits? Simply put, employers can be held liable for the criminal and/or torturous acts of their employees.

For example, let's suppose you hired a courtesy van driver and gave him a company car without bothering to check into his driving record, which would have shown he had a history of multiple drunk driving offenses. What do you think would happen if he had a few drinks at lunch, crashed your company vehicle into another vehicle and injured the other driver? It wouldn't be hard to argue that you were negligent in your hiring practices by not checking into his past driving record, and that you created a dangerous set of circumstances that put others at risk.

What if you ran a nursing home and people found out that a resident died because an employee was stealing their lifesaving drugs and selling them on the street? What if it was discovered after the fact that the same employee had a criminal record for stealing or selling drugs and you didn't bother to check?

The obvious benefit of performing background checks is to protect your company from negligent hiring lawsuits. Unfortunately, there are shortcomings with background checks, too. For example, a criminal background check only reveals that an individual was caught and successfully prosecuted. What about applicants who did things they weren't supposed to do but were never caught? Or what about those who were caught but weren't prosecuted? What about those who were prosecuted but weren't prosecuted successfully, even though they were guilty of committing the crimes?

I had a friend who was an executive at a beverage company representing the number two brand in a market. He told me about an incident where significant amounts of product (literally truckloads) had vanished over a period of time. As hard as the company tried, they couldn't identify the thief for quite some time, and losses continued to mount.

Eventually, they figured out that it had to be a long-term employee, because the thief had covered their tracks so successfully that it was obvious they had to know the company systems inside and out. It turned out that it was an employee who was nearing retirement. I asked if they called the police and escorted the thief through the building in handcuffs to send a message to the rest of the employees.

Do you want to guess what happened next? The answer is: nothing, except an early retirement party.

Why? It was because management realized that if they pressed charges, it would become public knowledge. Plus, it raised the potential threat that the number one brand leader in their market would exploit the issue to cause further distrust and customer dissatisfaction between my friend's company and the clients who didn't receive the beverages they purchased.

Even worse news is that the thief has a clean police record. They could apply to work at your company today, and a criminal background check wouldn't indicate that there was a problem at a previous employer.

The nature of my work has exposed me to situations like this quite frequently. They happen regularly, but the people they happen to are embarrassed and angry and don't want to admit it. Just because YOU don't hear about it all the time, that doesn't mean it isn't happening.

I recall a meeting I had with a vice president of sales for a construction company who had just fired a rep for stealing. He had hired that particular rep from a competitor.

The VP thought the rep was just looking to switch companies. Plus, the VP was attracted by the experience and contacts the rep said he had.

He THOUGHT he couldn't check references because he THOUGHT the rep was still employed by his competitor, when in fact the rep had already been fired for ... stealing! After firing the rep, the VP called the police, and they basically told him that because nobody was killed and drugs weren't involved, he should just let it go. So he did.

Guess what the rep who had just been fired from two companies did next? He listed the most recent VP as a reference on his resume for future employment consideration with other companies. When the VP was contacted for employment verification, the VP, for fear of being sued, would only agree to reveal employment dates and did not disclose the true reason for the rep's departure from his company.

Drug Testing

What about drug tests? Drug tests do catch individuals who have used drugs recently. It happens every day, and employers are wise to protect themselves from unnecessary risks. Unfortunately, most places of employment have a little sign on the reception desk letting applicants know that they will be tested for drugs. Also remember, drug testing must be conducted only after an initial offer of employment is extended to the applicant. So by the time you are drug testing the applicant, you have already selected them for the job and made them a conditional offer of employment.

What message does this send to applicants? It lets them know they need to stay clean for 30 days or until the traces of drugs are out of their system before applying for a job. If your company does hair tests, it means they need to stay clean for 90–120 days. Believe me, the word gets out in a community regarding which companies use which types of testing.

Reference Checks

Many employers still do perform reference checks. Occasionally, a person listed as a reference or previous employer will share their true feelings and let you know that a candidate is undesirable. But let's not pretend that applicants are often likely to give you names of people who will reveal the ugly truth about them.

Evaluating past experience leaves room for improvement, because 10 years of experience in the retail sporting goods industry might be more accurately described as one year of retail experience relived over and over 10 times. Previous employers are hesitant to give more than previous employment dates. Why? They don't want to reveal anything more because some of them are afraid of previous employees trying to sue them, or they want the terminated employee to get a new job and get off of unemployment, thus decreasing their unemployment premium liability.

Probation/Trial Periods

Trial periods and the use of temporary employees are popular screening methods and often work well for many companies. They are great ways for employers to observe the work performance of the new hire/temp before the company determines whether the person is a good fit or not. However, it is not beyond the imagination to see that some individuals (new hires/temps) put on a good act for 30, 60 or 90 days until they get hired on full-time. New hires have an extra incentive to put on a good show, especially if they know a union contract can protect, within certain parameters, their tardiness, absenteeism and/or absolute minimum output of discretionary effort once they are on full-time.

Assessments

As part of a complete selection process, I'm a fan of properly validated pre-employment assessments. If you're worried about getting sued for using them, well, you just need to accept the fact that you can get sued at any time for anything. Just ask McDonald's; they got sued for making coffee that was too hot.

However, when using a properly validated assessment that has been proven nondiscriminatory by age, race and sex as part of a complete, fair, thorough and consistent selection process (not the single reason for a hire/no hire decision), it might actually be your best DEFENSE against discrimination or unfair hiring practices. This is especially true because most are computer-scored and can't tell if someone is black, white, male, female or Martian.

I see tremendous value in basic skills assessments that measure things like basic math skills, vocabulary skills and spelling skills, as well as problem solving. In almost any job it is important to possess the basic learned skills required by a job.

I also see value in assessments and surveys that measure things like integrity, reliability, work ethic and attitudes toward substance abuse to help employers match the attitudes and values of applicants to the demands of jobs. They are a nice way to fill in the gaps left by background checks, drug tests and reference checks.

I see significant value in assessments that measure behavioral traits like assertiveness, flexibility, organization, social need, competitiveness, sensitivity, tension, etc., so employers can evaluate how a person does their job and whether or not it matches the behavioral requirements of the job. Behavioral assessments are a great way to complement interviews and help answer remaining questions afterward.

One of the biggest reasons why assessments are so effective at filling in holes left by other established selection processes is their ability to do one thing the others don't do well. What is it? The best assessments have built-in "distortion scores" or "lie scales" that alert employers whenever an individual may be trying to "fake good" or say what they think the employer wants to hear in order to get hired.

Think about it. How much easier would it be to take meaningful information out of an interview if you knew when applicants were lying and/or embellishing? It would make a night-and-day difference, wouldn't it? That's what a good "lie scale" or "distortion score" on a properly developed assessment tool does. It levels the playing field for the interviewer.

Overall – Be Consistent!

Whatever your hiring process looks like, it needs to be consistent. In other words, for every position you are trying to fill, the first step to the last step needs to be consistent in order to be fair.

Think about this example. Let's pretend that I am considering Johnny and Julie for the same position, but I've known Julie's family for 15 years and have personally known Julie since she was a little girl. The last steps in the established hiring process for this job are a background check and drug test. But because I know Julie and her family, I decide to hire Julie without administering a background check and drug test, even though I made Johnny jump through the hoops of a background check and drug test. Was this fair? No. Does Johnny have a legitimate claim? Yes. Why? It's because he was held to a more rigorous level of scrutiny.

Remember, whatever job you are filling, make sure your process is fair, thorough and consistent. Make sure it does not discriminate against any applicant based upon race, color, creed, gender, national origin, religious beliefs, sexual orientation, disability status, criminal history or veteran status. Of course, there may be an exception to the rule, but overall, you can never discriminate legally. If you complete your selection correctly, not only will this help protect you from a discrimination claim by a disgruntled applicant whom you didn't hire, but it will help defend your hiring practices in the event a government agency, such as the Equal Employment Opportunity Commission or the Office of Federal Contract Compliance Programs, decides to investigate your company's hiring practices.

Chapter 12:
Inventory Management System for Talent

Tony Robbins says, "Success leaves clues." I agree. How do you find them when it comes to your people?

Frank Sproule, an Atlanta-based business consultant, once told me, "If you don't know what made you a great team, how can you expect to continue the process?"

So how can you find out what made you a great team? How can you turn your human resource information into a corporate asset?

Step 1. Take Inventory of Your Human Assets (Assess Everyone)

Step 2. Identify Your Top Performers & Build Models That DEFINE Success for Each Position

Step 3. Hire, Develop and Manage in Ways That Minimize or Eliminate the Gaps

What if it were possible for you to create an inventory management system for your talent, just like many of you have for the products you have in your warehouses? What would it look like and how would it work?

Let me share an example of how this works. It was shortly after a furniture company opened its new corporate headquarters and warehouse, when one of the owners gave me a tour. We walked along the rows of shipping bays. While we were there, the docks were full of trucks and furniture was being unloaded in the bays and sent to specific locations within the main warehouse.

The owner showed me the nearby computer terminals and explained how the inventory management system operated in real time. For example, if a customer ordered a piece of furniture from one of their showrooms at a nearby location, even before it was unloaded from the truck, the system would immediately recognize the product and route it to the right outbound delivery truck without that piece of furniture ever being put into a specific slot in their warehouse.

If someone ordered a specific piece of furniture that was already being stored in their huge warehouse, the inventory management system could tell the forklift driver the row, shelf and specific slot where that piece of furniture was located, and do it instantly.

Can you imagine the chaos and time it would take to pick orders if they had no inventory management system? What if the forklift drivers had to try to remember where they, or one of the drivers, put a piece of furniture in a warehouse measuring the size of a football field and with shelves stacking 30 feet up to the ceiling?

Imagine what would happen if the forklift driver did not retrieve and ship out EXACTLY what the customer ordered and instead gave them something "close enough," in the opinion of the forklift driver. For example, what if the customer wanted black leather on the couch model they ordered, but the forklift driver thought blue might work just as well? Throw something that might be "close enough" up against the wall and see what your customer satisfaction survey results will be!

Of course, this doesn't happen all the time because product orders are specific and normally taken from a detailed catalog. But when it comes to filling positions from a pool of unknown external candidates, or even known internal candidates, far too many HR managers/recruiters are unaware of exactly what their customers (the department managers and supervisors needing a position filled) want. The HR managers/recruiters aren't sure if they have the correct internal or external candidates to fill their customers' vaguely defined requests. Too often, they throw a "close enough" applicant up against the wall to see what sticks.

And even if they DID know what their internal customers wanted in applicants, many HR managers/recruiters can't find them in their inventory of internal or external applicants quickly. Instead, they're digging around in stacks of paper and e-mails looking for what they thought they saw. To continue the analogy, this way of conducting talent management isn't that much different from wandering around in a warehouse looking for a piece of furniture among thousands of choices.

Applicant tracking systems can help IF the HR manager/recruiter knows EXACTLY what a job requires (in terms of knowledge, skills, attitudes/values and behaviors) and how well EVERY one of the internal and external candidates being considered matches those job requirements. Ideally, a system would exist that would correctly identify what each job requires and match both internal and external applicants automatically.

If you run or manage a small business, you might be thinking that you don't need an inventory management system for your products on the shelves, or an applicant tracking system to manage just a handful of applicants or employees. You may be right. But when it comes to determining what a job requires and whether or not your applicants match that job closely, it might be even MORE important that you get it right the first time than it is at a bigger company. Why? It's because companies like IBM are big enough that they could hire a thousand screwballs today and get them to blend in just fine over time while the other employees are covering for them.

If you have 500 employees or less, one single hiring disaster can ruin an otherwise successful organization. For example, if you're hiring a sales rep, what's the difference in annual sales production between what a top performer can produce and that of a gross underperformer? You might only get the opportunity to make that mistake once.

Maybe it isn't a sales position you're trying to fill. Maybe you need someone to work on a production line or in a warehouse as part of a team. Have no doubt, a single hiring mistake can cost a small fortune if the person steals, fakes injuries, brings the others' work output down to his/her level or initiates a gruesome workplace violence scenario (that creates a PR disaster and ruins your company's name and image).

Your ability to QUICKLY match an applicant (internal or external) to the demands of a job may be the ONLY strategic advantage you need. Wal-Mart created an empire with ONE strategic advantage (low prices); why can't you?

In a conversation with an HR manager of a company with about 1,000 employees in 15 locations, I asked how many positions they had open on any given day. She said 20% (about 200) were in the process of being filled at any given time.

Next, I asked her how long it took to fill the average position, because I knew their process was thorough. She said it was about 90 days.

I then asked her if there was anybody in the company who knew her job better than she did and told her to tell me the truth. Without hesitation and with confidence, she said there was nobody in the entire company who could do what she did as well as she did, or do it as quickly as she did.

I asked her how she would feel about coming back to work after one week of vacation if nobody checked her e-mails or voice mails, opened her mail or managed her inbox while she was gone. She liked the idea of taking a week off. Then I asked her how she would feel about coming back to work after two weeks in a row given the same circumstances. Then I asked her about three straight weeks. Then I asked her about a month.

She didn't want to imagine what kind of mess the untouched paperwork, e-mails and phone calls would create after just one month off the job, much less three. Then I reminded her that she was the most skilled, knowledgeable and experienced employee in the company at her job.

If she was the most capable person in the company in her role and couldn't imagine coming back to work after 90 days of abandonment, I asked her to consider the drag on corporate productivity caused by having 200 positions filled after 90-day vacancies by

BRAND-NEW people who didn't even know how to fill out their time cards yet and clearly WEREN'T the best at their job?

A great retention tool is to promote from within, and promoting from within sounds great to everyone (well, maybe not the HR manager/recruiter). Why? It's because there is something to be said for maintaining institutional knowledge. Hiring from within inspires people to work harder in their current role as if it was an audition for future promotions, not just doing their job in exchange for their current paycheck. It minimizes the learning curve compared to filling a position externally with someone who doesn't know the company's culture, purpose, business processes, etc. It also keeps people from taking the knowledge they've gained about YOUR company to your competitors. And these are just a FEW of the reasons.

And what about that HR manager/recruiter who doesn't like to promote from within? One of the main reasons people in HR/recruiting enjoy filling positions externally is that it can create MUCH less work for them, personally, during their hectic workweek.

Let me give you an example. Let's pretend that there is an opening at the executive level. If the position is filled externally, that means there is only one position to fill. If it is filled internally, then the HR manager needs to backfill the senior manager position that was vacated to fill the executive position. Then they have to backfill the middle manager position that was vacated to fill the senior manager position. Then they have to backfill the supervisor/entry level manager position that was vacated to fill the middle manager position and so on. It's a lot more work and takes a lot more time and resources. What would you rather do, fill one position or multiple ones with your limited time and resources?

But it doesn't have to be that way. The truth is that it is possible to backfill positions with internal candidates who match a job in 90 seconds or even 90 minutes instead of 90 days. Here's how.

Let's assume you visited http://www.ReverseRiskConsulting.com, became a client, and did the following:

1. Assessed all of your employees (behaviorally)

2. Built models of what each position required by analyzing the results of top performers in all of your key positions

3. Had an online inventory management system of your talent that allowed you to organize, search and evaluate job matches instantly

You could do a search within your database of employees to find out who best matched the behavioral requirements of the executive position and press a button to get your system to identify those best matching the demands of that job almost immediately. You could also remove those lacking the skill or required experience from consideration in as little as 90 seconds (or 90 minutes if you really wanted to take your sweet time). Simply repeat the process for the senior management position, the middle manager position and the supervisor/entry level management position.

With the correct inventory management system, you would have the best of both worlds. Just like the furniture chain knew what they had in inventory, where it was and exactly what their customers wanted so they could fill orders more efficiently, you could do the same with your

TALENT inventory (fill positions more accurately and quickly).

----

*NOTE: SUPER BONUS. As of the date of this printing, if you visit http://www.ReverseRiskConsulting.com and invest approximately 3–5 minutes answering some basic questions, it is likely that you can get the following tools entirely FUNDED for your company, regardless of size. It's basically an inventory management system for your talent. That's right. We are talking about potentially tens of thousands of dollars in savings delivered to you AT NO CHARGE and without any further obligation.

1. Online behavioral assessment of ALL of your employees – regularly $60 per person

2. A custom-built website (your inventory management system for your talent)

3. Training on how to utilize the data to evaluate the match between individuals and a job and tools to minimize conflict/improve relationships between individuals and their supervisors/leaders

When you are asked who referred you, be sure to mention this book title. If you think this offer sounds too good to be true, then fill out the questionnaire and see for yourself. What do you have to lose???

Chapter 13:
Relationship Management
(Employee/Supervisor)

That's enough about matching a person to the job, but what about the relationship between an employee and a specific supervisor?

Have you ever heard that old saying about how people don't quit the company, they quit their boss? Want to explore a way to solve that problem before it occurs? Try this: first gather data about the employee and their supervisor, and then probe more deeply to understand the relationship between the employee and their supervisor. This will allow you to make a more informed decision as it relates to conflict resolution and performance improvement.

There's a NO-COST function of the inventory management system for your talent I described earlier that allows you to do just that. (If you haven't filled out the application and evaluation form at http://www.ReverseRiskConsulting.com, I don't know what else to tell you.)

The function is called the Team Master (TM) report, and it compares a team member to a team leader in nine different dimensions of interaction:

1. Planning Needs

2. Use of Emotions

3. Communication Styles

4. Rules/Others' Emotions

5. Recognition Needs

6. Work Environment/Stress

7. Interaction with Others

8. Work Confrontations

9. Competitive Needs

Let's take the Rules/Others' Emotions dimension, for example. An individual may match the demands of a job just fine. However, suppose you're the team leader and you treat rules as gospel and expect everyone else to follow them to the letter. What's going to happen when you have a new team member who prides himself on flexibility and is happy to bend the rules (or ignore them) whenever he feels like it or thinks it is appropriate to do so?

Hint #1: You might want to discuss these dimensions of interaction by asking questions and discussing any issues that come up as soon as you hire someone and/or promote someone, especially if they are going to be working directly with you.

Hint #2: If an individual matches the demands of the job but might not be a good teammate for YOU, are there other executive or management peers of yours whom they would be better suited to work with? Does your executive or management peer have someone currently on their team who might be better suited to working with YOUR leadership style? With an inventory management system tool like the Team Master, you don't have to guess anymore.

Chapter 14:
Retention and Performance Improvement Strategies

Strategy #1 – Imprinting

I got this idea from Suanne Sandage (see http://www.ServicesForSuccess.com) when I was in Des Moines, Iowa. It's a strategy based on the power of self-fulfilling prophecy. Here's how it works.

Consider the background of a recent graduate entering the workforce.

In college, class attendance was encouraged, but it wasn't like having a job where students HAD to be there at all, much less on time. Unlike being forced to work a whole day straight at a job, if they partied too much or stayed out too late the night before, they had options to nap between classes. Maybe they skated through school easily without having to work too hard. Maybe everything came easily for them.

In any case, if you hire students right out of school, chances are good that you will spend a significant amount of time and money recruiting, screening and matching them to the job opening and the supervisor/manager in charge. A conservative estimate for most roles is that it will take at least three months for them to get really good at their new job and become a productive member of your team.

Three months is also long enough for people who are struggling in their new position to question whether or not they made the right decision accepting your offer. It is also within the window of time when the other companies the new hire reached out to during their initial job search are still interested in the new hire and may continue to reach out to them. So if things don't go the way the new hire had hoped, the "grass might look greener" and the new hire might consider taking a position with another company BEFORE they ever really are fully trained or start earning their keep at YOUR company.

This is the worst time to lose good people, especially when they DO match the demands of the job and the leadership style of their team leader. Why? Because your investment in recruiting and training them has yet to pay off.

What I'm about to suggest isn't likely to help you retain all of your new hires, but what if it could help you save one-third, or even one-half, of them? What if I could suggest a conversation that might only take a few minutes of your time and yet would set forth a self-fulfilling prophecy that would increase your probability of retaining your new hires AND improve their performance while they are there? But before you have this conversation, you need to consider when it should take place. You should have this conversation on their first day on the job or as soon as possible.

All you need to do is pull out your behavioral profile that compares the new hire to their job pattern. Then explain the following using your own words or something similar to what I'm about to share with you.

"Mr. New Hire, I want to welcome you to ABC Company. We're glad you're here. As you know, our selection process was quite exhaustive. We evaluated your application, resume, references, background and attitude toward drugs, work ethic and more. We

compared you to all kinds of outstanding people, and we picked you.

"I'd like you to know why. You see, we know what it takes to succeed in all of the key roles of our company. We analyzed the role we selected you for, and numerous other key positions, to determine exactly what the role required of individuals likely to perform EXTREMELY well. We did this based on scientific research and analysis of PROVEN top performers in each of those roles.

"First of all, as you can see here, the job you were selected for requires the following, and look how closely you fit. (Then show them the results from their behavioral assessment, and highlight what the job requires and how closely they match the job requirements. You might even point out a few areas where they fell a bit outside of your ideal target, but were close. Then suggest ways you can surround the new hire with people, tools, systems or technologies to compensate or help them overcome the gaps.)

"Because you so closely match the scientific models of our top performers, I'm confident that you have what it takes to do an outstanding job here, as long as you continue to seek more knowledge and put forth the effort to apply *what you have learned. It won't always be easy, but you are built for whatever challenges this job will provide you with.*

"Second, here are the models of other positions in this company that you would also be a good fit for later on down the road, assuming you put forth the effort necessary and demonstrate the characteristics we hired you for. At all times I want you to remember that you are not just being evaluated for your current position, but you're also auditioning your candidacy for these other roles, too. When other roles open up, we know who fits them. So, when the time is right and you have the experience necessary, you won't have to politic around here to get considered; your performance will speak for itself.

"Do your best. Seek experience and develop your knowledge and skills. Stick it out, even if it gets tough, and great things are possible for you here."

If you have a conversation with a new hire like the one above, then:

1. You have set forth a self-fulfilling prophecy; the new hire will want the prophecy to come true.

2. If the new hire struggles in the first three to six months, they might be more likely to "stick it out" if they have a reason to believe it will be worth it.

3. The new hire is likely to put forth a greater portion of their "discretionary effort" if they consider themselves as auditioning for future promotions.

Strategy #2 – Conflict Resolution

Conflict kills productivity. It distracts people. It scares them. It hurts their feelings.

Some people will quit their jobs, move their families and risk financial ruin to avoid confrontation. Others will avoid contributing to the success of their rivals. And some will even sabotage their rivals, hurting the company in the process, if they think they can get away with it.

When people are hurting, they want change. When they aren't being listened to, don't feel their contributions are being valued and lack the mechanisms in place to make their pain go away, they often turn to lawyers, the media, social media or union representation, or perhaps all of these, to fix things. The good news is, it doesn't have to be that way.

What if I told you that one of the easiest, fastest and most inexpensive solutions to conflict resolution was hiding in plain sight? What if I told you that you and your managers don't have to do much, if any, additional work? What if you just had to do a better job with something that you all should be doing, and probably are doing, on a regular basis already?

Let's talk about performance appraisals and reviews. If you're a leader, do you like giving performance appraisals? Are you good at giving them? How do you know? Do the employees receiving the appraisal improve their performance significantly? If so, do they sustain the improved effort and results?

In most cases, honest managers will tell you that it seems like a waste of time to conduct performance appraisals and reviews, unless they are merely documenting employee shortcomings to justify the act of firing an individual later. (Note: Most HR managers will tell you that you should be using the disciplinary process to justify and document the events leading up to an individual's termination, not a performance appraisal.)

What if there was an easy way to improve the discretionary effort of your employees during the performance appraisal process? You have to do it anyway, so you might as well make your life a little better, too, don't you think? What if it could be accomplished in a nonthreatening way so as to not escalate existing animosity? What if it could reduce conflict and the risk of unnecessary firings, lawsuits and employee drama that distract OTHER workers from focusing on THEIR jobs?

Frank Sproule, a consultant friend of mine in Atlanta, once asked me three questions that I never forgot. I'm going to share them with you and ask that you reflect on the answers, as I did the first time I heard them.

1. Have you ever been mismanaged?

2. What was your productivity like during that period of time?

3. Did the person who was mismanaging you make any effort to fix the problem?

When I think of my own personal experience, I have been mismanaged. I know my productivity was good enough not to get fired, but my effort was nowhere near the maximum potential of what I was capable of delivering on any given day. The person who was mismanaging me only made things worse, and it felt like "no good deed went unpunished" when I did put forth extraordinary (but unnecessary) effort.

Perhaps you can relate?   Perhaps your subordinates can relate?

Consider this next scenario as a model for how you could set the stage for your next performance appraisal. If you use your own words and a tool like the Team Master report, you can become capable of a conversation like the one that follows.

Scenario: Let's pretend that you have a technician and a supervisor at XYZ Company. The technician works in the field, directly interacting with customers, and reports to the supervisor, who manages an entire team of people just like him. It is time for performance appraisals by the supervisor, who, by the way, USED to be in the field working with customers directly, doing the same job the technicians do now, and was promoted to his supervisor role just a few years ago.

Let's also assume the supervisor has gotten a bit "comfortable" in the new role and spends most of his time at his desk, with very little interaction with his team members unless there are problems that require his attention. It's not hard to imagine some animosity and/or resentment building up among the team members in the field. You could also presume the field technicians have solved and prevented all kinds of problems the supervisor never even knew about, but WOULD have known about if the supervisor ever left the comfort of his office and went out into the field. How receptive do you think the technicians would be to "coaching" and advice on how to improve in their jobs from the guy hiding in the office trying to micromanage them?

It's not hard to predict that most, if not all, of the technicians would sit there and listen to whatever the supervisor had to say, nod their heads in agreement and bite their tongues, so as to not aggravate the supervisor and jeopardize their job security or risk any possibility of losing a pay raise. They might even go out and apply the supervisor's advice for a short while until the supervisor became distracted with other stuff, allowing things to go back to "normal" (meaning everyone returning to doing just enough so as not to get fired).

Now, returning to the Team Master report tool that was referred to earlier, it's obvious that there are lots of dimensions that can be explored on that particular tool. Let's just look at one, as an example, and I'll shed some light on how the information can be applied in a real-life scenario.

For the sake of discussion, let's assume that the Team Master report indicates the following on the PLANNING NEEDS dimension.

The supervisor:

1. dislikes emergencies

2. detests chaos and believes everything has its place

3. likes to work in a step-by-step fashion

4. hates unplanned changes

5. demands structure and strict adherence to rules

6. will only delegate comfortably to people who have the same respect for order

7. prefers established methods

8. will clamp down on team members to force attention to details

The technician:

1. can easily change directions with little advance notice

2. considers details of work to be a low priority

3. prefers to look for new ways of doing things

4. likes to have "room to roam" and dislikes overly structured environments

Clearly, the probability of stress between these two people in this dimension is VERY high.

As an example of how I would initiate the performance appraisal process if I were the supervisor in possession of the Team Master report, I'd say something like this to the technician:

"Mr. Technician, as you know, it's time for our annual review. I want to acknowledge that you help a lot of our customers, and you help me, too, even though it seems most of our interaction is tied to challenges when they come up. It's the unfortunate nature of the job that I had to deal with, too, when I was a field

technician and had your responsibilities. So, I understand what it's like out in the field.

"I'd like to address the things you do well so I can continue to get you the support you need. Plus, I'd like to discuss any potential opportunities for improvement that either of us uncover, so you can get the support you need there as well.

"However, before we begin, I'd like to talk about our relationship first. I'm not perfect. I don't expect you to be either. I do think it's important for both of us to identify and talk about any potential blind spots we might have in our working relationship and fix them if we can.

"The obvious question is, how? I've got an idea, and I hope you don't mind playing along and going through this exercise with me so I can see if it helps. It might work or it might not, but I'm willing to give it a shot if you are.

"Remember when we took that behavioral assessment, back in the day, to help our organization build models identifying what it took to be successful in various positions in our company so we could hire more effectively in the future? Well, it turns out that one byproduct of that process is a report we can run that is supposed to shed light on our relationship and expose any blind spots that EITHER of us might have in our working relationship.

"I don't know how accurately it will describe what it's like for the two of us to work together, but I'm curious to see what it says. I'm not willing to take what it says as gospel without looking at it WITH you, so we can both be the judge as to whether or not there's any merit to it."

(Both the supervisor and the technician should review the report at this time.)

"After reading this report, it says that you need mental room to roam and you dislike highly structured environments. It says I tend to clamp down on you and force you to pay attention to details you may consider unnecessary, and that this could be a source of friction between us."

At this point, the supervisor needs to be quiet and listen to what the technician says. Why? Because what the technician says will help guide the discussion. Here are some examples of questions the supervisor may ask to get more feedback from the technician.

IMPORTANT QUESTION #1: "Is there some accuracy to this report?"

If the technician says "yes" and acknowledges a source of friction in their relationship, the following question needs to be asked. It should be asked in an inquisitive, rather than defensive, manner.

IMPORTANT QUESTION #2: "Can you give me some specific examples of the friction?"

One of two things will happen:

1. The technician says something like this:

"Do you remember when you put me in charge of that one project over the 4th of July? Well, I realized after the event that you redid the schedules I created, and you determined which vendors we would use. You also established the terms and parameters under which their products and services would be provided. You also created and insisted that they sign Memorandums of Understanding, detailing specific consequences should they fail to perform to the standards you considered acceptable. God knows, I got at least 35 voice mails and another 25 e-mails related to

that day. You got involved to the point that you specified what kind of signs and banners we would use at the event, including the colors, materials and types of fonts.

"Given that the event was just a family picnic for the people in our department, and the whole purpose was to get everyone to enjoy visiting and spending time together, I felt your need for control and micromanagement was a bit over the top based on the nature of the activity. But you're the boss, so I just kept my mouth shut and went with it.

"You could have just told me we needed a picnic planned for our department members and families, and things would have turned out fine, too. Perhaps they would have been different than you might have planned, but it doesn't necessarily mean worse. I mean, really, how hard is it to pick a place and arrange for food, drinks, some music and a few activities, especially when you already know most of the people and have a good idea about the things they like?"

What this response means:

Maybe the technician can list a few other examples. In any case, it's a good bet that the supervisor got his eyes opened to a blind spot in his behavioral tendencies. The net outcome is that the supervisor received valuable feedback that eliminated a blind spot and allowed him to grow professionally. It's likely that the supervisor will become better at his job because of this feedback and the technician will be inclined to perform at a higher level, too.

Why?

a. The supervisor became aware of his own mismanagement style (and now can stop doing it).

b. The technician's "voice" regarding his wants and needs was heard by his supervisor, and when they are heard, people tend to give more discretionary effort because there is less animosity toward their supervisor.

2. In other situations, the technician might say this:

"You know ... now that I really think about it. I can't give you a specific example."

What this response means:

It means the supervisor may INTEND to control and micromanage every chance he gets, and the technician senses it. The technician may be harboring animosity because he "felt" the supervisor's DESIRE to force rules and structure upon him, even though the supervisor's ACTIONS may not have been unreasonable.

But here's where the "aha" moment comes to the technician. He realizes his animosity toward his supervisor may be misplaced given that he can't produce a single specific example of the egregious behavior he "felt" before. It's a reasonable explanation that the supervisor in this scenario may have recognized his overwhelming desire for order, adherence to rules and certainty. It's also a reasonable explanation that the supervisor has intentionally and conscientiously given people who work for him the space they need, whenever possible, even if it's uncomfortable.

At this point it's possible, maybe even probable, that the technician "cuts the boss some slack" and feels better about working for him because "he's not such a bad guy" after all.

In the first response, the company wins because the supervisor will become better at what he does based on the feedback from the technician, and the technician will become more willing to deliver more discretionary effort because of it.

In the second response, the company also wins. It's just for different reasons. The supervisor receives positive reinforcement for modifying his behavior to suit his team members as necessary. The technician becomes more willing to unleash extra doses of discretionary effort because he stops placing animosity where it doesn't belong, becoming more willing to "help" his supervisor.

The beauty of this approach lies in establishing the report as the "thing" the supervisor and technician will evaluate, enabling them to judge their insights TOGETHER. They both get to discuss what they believe is and isn't accurate and explain why. They work together to judge the characterizations found in an independent third-party document, which is MUCH less confrontational (and significantly more useful) compared to a situation where an employee is being judged by a supervisor and feels forced to defend himself or herself.

Strategy #3 – Targeting Training, Development and Support Needs

What are you REALLY good at doing? Where do you REALLY excel? What knowledge, skills, abilities or talents do people go out of their way to compliment you on?

Conversely, what are you terrible at doing? What knowledge, skills, abilities or underdeveloped skills cause others to criticize or embarrass you when showcased in public?

In what kind of work environment would you produce the most value? Would it be an environment that relied on frequent performance of duties that regularly showcased and relied on the things you were best at and liked doing the most? Or would you rather work in a role that depended on the performance of duties and tasks that you weren't good at and that caused everyone to notice your flaws?

What's the take-away? It's that people perform better in jobs that suit them. People also tend to stay in those jobs longer.

Dr. Barbara Carnes, author of the book *Making Training Stick*, once told me, "If you don't have a standard, how can you expect to measure the deviation?" When you have assessed top performers in all of your key positions and developed behavioral models of what each job requires, those standards not only are used as models for hiring but can and should be used for targeting training, developmental and support needs of staff, too. The bigger the deviation and the more places it occurs between an individual and the demands of a job, the more managerial effort and expense will be tied to improving performance and retaining the individual placed in that role.

Good applicants and employees will match the behavioral requirements of a job pretty closely. In an effort to transform a GOOD employee into a GREAT one, simply look at the gaps between what a job requires and what that person brings to the job, and ask one simple question: "What tools, systems, training, people or technologies are needed to support the individual to compensate for those gaps?"

I readily admit that the Achilles heel to better performance in my role is related to my organizational skills. For years I tried to make up for my lack of them with exceptional imagination, flexibility and problem-solving skills.

I have shown up to meetings without business cards. I have shown up to presentations without my laptop and projector adapters. One time, I found myself in Minneapolis, 10 hours away from home. It was 90 minutes before I was supposed to give a presentation to all the top executives of a 14-location corporation, when, while I was getting ready at my hotel, I realized that my suit pants had fallen off the hanger and were still lying on the bottom of my closet at home. (Thankfully, one of my triathlon buddies lived close by in Woodbury, Minnesota, and happened to be the same size as I am. I called him and borrowed one of his suits. How's that for flexibility, imagination and problem solving?)

I'm good at my job, even with my Achilles heel. However, I'm MUCH better at my job with the help of specific people, tools and technologies. For example, I don't have to worry about organizing my e-mail folders or files because of the search engines in my e-mail systems. I can also access all of my important contact information, as well as the Internet, from my smartphone. And I now have an assistant to help me with important details I used to miss.

What's the payoff? If you're a manager, your job security and income aren't always tied to the technical aspects of a job you are supposed to be leading others to perform. You will be judged by the quality and output of the work OTHERS provide under your direction.

You need to identify the gaps and the deviations from your ideal targets. The more gaps there are, and the wider they are from what the job requires, the more time, resources and management attention will be required to compensate for those gaps.

If you are a manager, then do yourself a favor and make informed and targeted selection and management decisions when it comes to the strengths and weaknesses of the people surrounding you. You've got a lot invested in your career. This is one of the best ways to protect that investment.

Strategy #4 – David Rock's S.C.A.R.F. Model

In the 1920s, Walter Cannon described two physiological reactions to perceived threats. One reaction was to flee or get away (flight). The other was to resist or overcome the threat (fight).

Some people can't stand the companies they work for and leave (flight). Others can't stand the companies they work for and would rather fight to change them. When enough people want to fight and they don't think they can do it by themselves, they often seek help from third parties (lawyers, media outlets, labor unions, etc.).

In addition to some of the tools and strategies we have already discussed, there are some things EVERY manager can do to keep employees from feeling threatened unnecessarily. Years ago, I became a fan of a thought leader named David Rock. He coined the "S.C.A.R.F." model as a way of pinpointing common factors capable of producing "threat states" in employees. Every manager or leader of others would be well served, in my opinion, to remain aware of these threat-inducing factors and adjust their behaviors and words accordingly. So, what does S.C.A.R.F. stand for? It stands for:

- **S**tatus

- **C**ertainty

- **A**utonomy

- **R**elatedness

- Fairness

Let's look at each factor in more detail, and in particular, their relationship to how unions can come into play.

Status

According to the *Merriam-Webster Dictionary* (http://www.merriam-webster.com), the definition of *status* is "Position or rank in relation to others." The bigger the perceived gap in status between management and employees (the more employees feel diminished in comparison), the more uncomfortable and in need of change (flight) or help (from unions) they are likely to feel.

Let me give you an example. Although assisted living communities are a component under the "health care" umbrella, I truly believe that assisted living is so much more than what we used to think of as nursing homes. The "residents" of assisted living communities today are different from their peers of past generations. (I put quotation marks around the word *resident* because the people who pay to live in assisted living complexes are more like "owners," especially when you consider the average price for a room and the services they receive.)

For past generations, relocating to a nursing home facility was akin to going somewhere to live out the remaining days of your life, and where death was close by. However, today's generation of seniors has a different perspective on growing older, and the idea of entering a senior living facility has totally changed from that of a nursing home to a vibrant senior citizen community.

Today's generation of seniors has the viewpoint that living in an assisted living community is like moving into a new home. They want the same freedoms and amenities that they enjoyed in their previous home. They are not moving to an assisted living community to die; instead, they are moving there to live and to enjoy their time with a community of people who have needs and wants similar to theirs. They want to maximize their freedom and relationships, all while having their needs met by a dedicated staff of medical professionals, care managers, dining staff and housekeepers.

It is the dedicated staff, and in particular the care managers, dining staff and housekeepers, that I would like to focus on now.

Care managers take care of the owners (residents) who require additional support. This support may include taking care of their bathing and personal needs, almost as if the owner was an extended member of the care manager's own personal family. The care manager is ultimately responsible for the total administration of care and support for the owner (resident) in the absence of the medical staff.

Who is caring for the care manager?

What about the dining staff? Not only are they responsible for knowing the dietary likes and dislikes of the owners (residents), but they need to make sure every breakfast, lunch and dinner is served properly and on time.

Dining staff members are also frequent recipients of what I like to refer to as the "Jell-O smear." The "Jell-O smear" occurs when an owner (resident) decides against the cherry Jell-O that has been served that day and decides to throw it at the nearest dining staff member.

The professional dining staff member is forced to regroup and resist the urge to say anything impolite. Instead, they quietly head to the locker room to clean up.

Understandably, they are humiliated, hurt and embarrassed, and may even be angry and wanting to take some form of revenge. However, they can't bring themselves to hurt someone so old or risk losing their job because of their own personal responsibilities back at home.

Who is there to reinstate the dining staff member's sense of worth ... or confidence?

What about the housekeeping staff? They are often the invisible employees. They push their carts up and down the hallways all day. They do a job that few of them aspired to when they were younger. They clean the rooms of owners (residents), who only acknowledge the housekeeping staff exists when their chair isn't dusted to their exact specifications, something is out of place in their bedrooms or something is missing.

Who makes the housekeepers feel visible and worthwhile? Who pats them on the back after a long, hard day?

The logical answer to "who is caring for the care manager," "who is there to reinstate the sense of worth and confidence for members of the dining staff" and "who pats the housekeepers on the back after a hard day of work" is: their manager. Unfortunately, this is not always the case.

Just as the employees work hard to meet the needs of the owners (residents), the managers are often working just as hard to make sure their departments function properly, despite the fact that the managers usually have limited resources and time.

As a result, the support needs of individual staff members don't often get met. Instead of offering empathy and support, busy managers have been known to ignore their cries and respond with what one might call shallow pep talks. For example, a manager may say, "Why are you crying? Try doing my job. Pick yourself up and get back out there." An employee can only take so many of these shallow encounters before they become hardened, indifferent and tired of having their status diminished by their manager.

Employee commitment suffers, and staff members begin doing the minimum necessary to keep their jobs and paychecks coming. Their hearts and minds are elsewhere.

To that care manager or housekeeping or dining staff member, the MANAGER who doesn't have time for them, belittles them or ignores them has become part of the problem. The union can be made to seem like a viable solution. This is the window of opportunity that union organizers look for and capitalize on whenever they get the chance.

Certainty

Certainty is the absence of doubt and a feeling of confidence. When people don't know what is happening in an organization or why, it is easy for them to become fearful of that which they do not understand. Companies who keep employees in the dark when forcing change, without communicating the reasons, are inviting unpleasant (fight-or-flight) consequences.

For example, several years ago a company came under attack from a local union. It turned out that the corporate officers of this company had forced significant changes to warehouse policies without asking the managers of that facility for input.

Because the managers were forced to execute these policies without input, they, in turn, forced their employees to execute these policies without input. Managers would say things to employees like, "I know you don't want to do this. We don't want to do it either. But corporate is forcing us to do this, so get to work."

When employees tried to voice concerns about unpleasant potential consequences, offer input or request additional training, managers who felt pressure from the corporate officers barked back. The managers told them to do what they were told or they'd have to get people in there who would. The "threat state" felt by the employees opened the door to the union.

Autonomy

You want to believe that you were hired for your job because your employer or manager has faith in you. So do the people who work for you. If given the choice, micromanaged employees may be inclined to leave their job (flight) or change their job (fight) using the help of a third party (union).

Don't micromanage. Give people adequate time, tools, training and support to accomplish assigned tasks safely and properly. If you don't, you are putting employees in a "threat state," and it is unnecessary.

Relatedness

People like and are more inclined to trust other people they "feel" are like them. This is where diversity training and initiatives make a difference. Diversity is not just about age, sex or race. Reasons why people relate (or not) to others can include things like educational level, musical tastes, recreational activities, hometown, favorite pro sports teams and more. If some groups or subgroups of employees can't find ways to relate to management, common work objectives or anything else, then prepare for fight-or-flight reactions. But the best advice is to do something about it before it is too late!

I know an innovative CEO who understands how to go about finding what we call the "emotional levers" of the people who work for her. She knows how to find out what makes people tick. She invests whatever time is necessary to understand and relate to the people who work in her organization.

If she doesn't know how to relate to someone, she asks questions until she finds out. She asks questions such as:

- "What do you think about on your way to work?"

- "What do you think about on your way home from work?"

- "While you're at work, what do you need in order to do your job?"

- "What's your favorite part of living in the area?"

She owns 40 assisted living facilities around the country and gives each employee her personal cell phone number. Each year, she travels to each facility and meets with the employees in small focus groups. During these focus groups meetings, she'll spend 5 minutes of her time talking and the next 55 minutes listening.

It's hard to relate to people you don't know or talk to. It is also hard for people to be able to relate to you if you don't give them the chance to get to know more about you.

Fairness

Everyone wants to feel they are being given a fair shake. Nobody likes to feel like they are being taken advantage of. Making the effort to fairly reward, acknowledge and celebrate people's contributions, as well as addressing any perceived discrepancies, will go a long way toward lasting and prosperous employee/management relationships.

I've had employment lawyers tell me that the easiest way to prevent employment-related lawsuits is to treat people fairly. I've had public relations professionals point out how companies could have avoided being embarrassed in the media if they had only been more sensitive to an employee who felt "wronged" by them. I've seen companies become unionized because a majority of the people felt the company they worked for took advantage of them.

Be fair. Be nice. It's not hard. It's not expensive. Actually, it's just common sense.

CONCLUSION

The relationship between employers and employees has been dissected, studied under the microscope and debated for decades by government officials, scholars, consultants, union leaders and business leaders. Most of the time, this relationship is viewed as an "us versus them" relationship when, in fact, it should be viewed as a "let's work together so we can both be successful" relationship.

To help ensure a positive relationship exists between employers and employees, employers must first understand what the requirements of the job are, as well as the culture of the organization. Once employers understand these requirements, they can then start to recruit and hire those applicants who match the requirements. And as we have talked about in this book, there are solid, validated assessment tools that can be used to help identify the right applicants for the right jobs.

However, hiring applicants with the right assessment results won't guarantee a successful relationship will exist. Besides getting the "right employee," employers must also make sure they get the right employee in the "right seat." And once the employee is in the "right seat," the employer must dedicate the time and resources to train, and continue to train, the employee to be successful at their job.

But there is even more to the building of successful employer–employee relationships. The employer, and in particular the first-line supervisor/manager, must treat all employees with respect and dignity, as well as providing a safe working environment that includes a competitive wage, challenging job duties, opportunities to contribute and be promotable and the ability to communicate with management when the need arises.

Communicate. It doesn't sound like it would be hard to communicate with someone. All you have to do is open your mouth and let the words spew out. Unfortunately, out of all the competencies employees are evaluated on, the ability to effectively communicate is probably the hardest one to master. Why? Why is it so difficult to communicate?

There are many reasons why it is difficult to communicate with someone else. If you think about how you communicate at home, you are usually less formal, it's easier to share ideas and you don't normally fear something bad is going to happen to you if you say something bad. (Okay, that's not always true. I know my teenage twins are very hesitant to tell me the "bad" stuff. I guess I'm too strict. So they go to their mother, who, in turn, will tell me what's going on and get my initial response.) It's also easier to communicate at home because those involved already know each other very well. They know what will upset someone and what will make someone happy. Plus, at home, you pretty much know that you won't get "fired" from the family, just sent to your room, if the news is really bad.

Communicating at work is much different. You may not know the people you have to communicate with very well, if at all. And many times in the workplace, the communication process involves presenting bad and unwelcome news. So, how can you be successful at work with people you hardly know?

To be successful, you must be able to relate to the person you are communicating with. This includes using your listening skills, understanding where the other person is coming from and acknowledging what the other person is saying – without judging their opinions. Simply put, this is showing empathy.

To be empathetic, not only must you understand others, but you must also understand yourself. By this I mean you must know yourself: your biases, your prejudices, your beliefs, your values and your emotional triggers that distract you from thinking rationally. Remember the old saying about walking in someone else's moccasins before you judge them? That's what I am referring to here. Before you judge someone's ideas or suggestions, make sure you understand why they are telling you these things. Maybe, just maybe, they know more about the situation you are discussing because they are closer to it than you are and are being directly impacted by it.

But be warned! If you don't listen to your employees ... if you don't show them empathy ... if you don't treat them with dignity and respect, then someone else will. And guess who that someone else will be? Correct. It will be a third-party representative who will give them these considerations. And to make your work environment even more challenging, your employees will pay this third-party representative to force you to give them the considerations they want.

Let me leave you with this one thought: Successful organizations rely heavily on the relationships between management and the employees. This is called positive employee relations. Unfortunately, when the relationship between management and the employees sours, and most of the time it is the result of "piss-poor management" (sorry for my bluntness), then a third party enters the picture and the relationship (now called labor relations) looks like this:

management ↔ third-party representative ↔ employees

Don't let this happen to you. Treat your coworkers with dignity and respect. Go beyond the ability to hear what they are saying. Listen to them. Understand why they do what they do and say what they say, and do so with empathy. Invest time and effort into the relationships you have with your coworkers.

It's funny, but everyone acknowledges the fact that we spend more time with our "work family" than we do with our own family back home. So why don't we take the time and effort to get to know our "work family" like we do with our own family? If you don't, someone else will!

About the Authors

Mason Duchatschek

Mason Duchatschek is a #1 Amazon.com bestselling author, keynote speaker and consultant (http://www.MasonDuchatschek.com). His ideas have been featured in *Selling Power* magazine, *The New York Times*, *Entrepreneur* magazine, *Newsweek*, Fox News and numerous other national media outlets.

He is also the president of AMO - Employer Services, Inc. (http://www.ReverseRiskConsulting.com). He is a business expert and thought leader who knows how to solve common business problems before they occur, particularly as they relate to employee selection, development and retention.

As a volunteer, he served as the president of the Human Resource Management Association of St. Louis. He also served on the Missouri State

Council for the Society of Human Resource Management (SHRM).

Mason is also a former U.S. Army officer, Official Guinness World Record Holder and experienced endurance athlete who has successfully completed multiple Ironman triathlons and a 100-mile ultra-marathon.

Jason Greer

Jason Greer is founder and president of Greer Consulting, Inc. (GCI), a labor and employee relations consulting firm (http://www.GreerConsultingInc.com). His ideas and strategies have been featured in *The Wall Street Journal*, *Forbes*, Fox News and The British Broadcasting Corporation (BBC).

He started his career as a board agent with the National Labor Relations Board, where he managed private sector labor relations issues and worked to improve the labor petition filing process. Jason currently helps large and small businesses across multiple industries overcome their internal employee relations and diversity-related struggles.

His background in labor relations, counseling psychology and organizational development make him one of the most sought-after labor consultants in the United States. His stories and dynamic presentation skills have made him one of the most sought-after keynote speakers as well.

Ken Lynch, SPHR, SHRM-SCP

Ken Lynch has been in the HR field for over 35 years and is currently a vice president of human resources with a major foodservice distributor. He is also an adjunct full professor for a global university, where he has facilitated the professional development of hundreds of HR professionals over the past 15 years.

He also contributes his expertise to several nonprofit organizations, from volunteering on their HR committees to sitting on the Board of Directors. In addition to mentoring HR professionals in the field, Ken sponsors two HR resources: the HR Diner (www.hrdiner.com) and the HR Network. As a veteran of the U.S. Army, Ken is active in assisting veterans with their transition back to the civilian workforce.

Ken has been a guest speaker and trainer on leadership development, labor relations and employment law. He holds an undergraduate degree in psychology and a graduate degree in business administration and is completing a doctoral degree program in management.

64272747R00080

Made in the USA
Lexington, KY
02 June 2017